Master Time

Volume 1

Master Time

Volume 1

by Ace Doligosa

GOKUREN PUBLISHING
2020

Dedicated to all the people who supported me and survived COVID-19 with me through every trial. Thank you.

Table of Contents

Preface 11

Intro 12

Author's Encouragement Note 16

Month Plan 18

Week 1 22

Week 2 38

Week 3 54

Week 4 70

Week 5 86

Vision and Goals 102

Notes 105

About Author 115

Preface

This planner was inspired by an article I read called "How to Master Time". In this article, SGI President Daisaku Ikeda explains: "Everyone has the same 24 hours in a day. However, if you use those hours wisely, you can accomplish a week's worth of effort in a day, or 10 years' worth of effort in a year. I have lived my life with that spirit." (Jan. 1, 2016, World Tribune, p. 8)

About a year ago, I went from a 9am-6pm job to setting my sights on becoming an entrepreneur. In those days of floundering and setting my foundation, I was fortunate enough to come across people like Neil Strauss, Kash Raston, and a slew of successful LA artists. They all had this burning desire to make it on their own outside of the normal desk job. With them as my example and with the help of an amazing life coach I designed the appropriate schedule for myself. I sustained an energized spirit by listening to motivational speakers and reading self-help books to keep me focused on my goals and determined to accomplish them.

Through all these efforts, I was able to create this self-help motivational planner for you.

When Covid19 hit, I learned that many people also floundered with the same feeling of instability as job opportunities disintegrated and work at home became the norm. To help clarify and strengthen one's own determination to succeed in any field, I created this motivational, life coach planner to help provide the structure.

As you read on and use this planner, I hope you see it as a helpful anchor to which you constantly refer when the days get tough. And, that you enjoy it as a keepsake reminder of your cumulative efforts and accomplishments.

Introduction

Welcome to your one-stop-shop motivational planner. *Master Time* is your own life coach, planner, and motivator all in one place. Please note, I still recommend investing in a human life-coach in conjunction with this planner. That one-to-one personal connection between you and a person who motivates you and holds you accountable to achieve your goals is a powerful resource to have that will take you from 0 -100% efficiency. It will also free up your conversations to talk about less work at home. Let me show you how this thing works with a few sample pages.
(See the next page...)

Let's talk about scheduling for the week. As you plan your weeks by creating the space for the following activities, you will be able to keep a balanced rhythm in between social, recreational, and work. I recommend taking 30 minutes of quiet time to fill out this page on Sunday afternoon so that you may jump into the Monday with a clear head. The goal here is to plan out as much as you can ahead of time so that you can move through your week with ease.
(See page 14...)

I have placed the Vision and Goals section at the end of the book. Without a proper vision for myself and my future, I tended to move aimlessly throughout the drudgery of a purposeless life. It's important to set time aside to properly envision who you want to be in a year, ten years, and thirty years, etc. I'm on the young side of life but, through conversations with my mentors, parents, and family members, I've accepted their advice. Life passes by in a blink of an eye and as we get older time move faster. One day, you can end up in a place you never thought you would be and freak out because you forgot where you wanted to go.

This vision, this dream that you create, is possible. What's important is that you remain flexible and you revise it as much as possible. Some of the highest performing individuals revise their life vision every day. In this book you have the space to start your vision and in the next volume, you can revise your vision. The goal here is to live your happy, fulfilling life. It's more possible than you think.

See Page 102 (Visions and Goals)

Weekly Plan

1. Plan 45-Minute Daily conditioning workouts to keep you feeling strong

True strength comes from your ability to decide and commit. The physical conditioning is what provides practice and the refinement of your inner strength.

SUN	MON	TUE	WED	THU	FRI	SAT
• legs • cardio	• Chest 5x5 • Triceps	• Upper abs • Oblique	• Back • Shoulders	• Upper Chest • Biceps	• Back • Shoulders	• Plyometric • Triceps

2. Plan 3 calls each day to feel connected and mitigate the risk of isolation & depression

A simple, "How are you doing?" or "Hey! Letting you know I'm alive," starts the conversation. We are not alone, and we can break through feelings of loneliness by caring for others.

SUN	MON	TUE	WED	THU	FRI	SAT
• Mom • Debbie • Alfred	• Ian • Ezra • Jen	• Chris G. • Billy Bob • Nick	• Kat V. • Annabelle • Adam	• Ian • Anita D. • Ezra	• Mom • Uncle Chris • Aunt Debbie	• Mcloven • Gabe's mom • Joey

3. Plan 3 activities a week for fun

We can't just keep working. We need moments of Joy!—to be good to others and to ourselves. Schedule a dance class or a jackbox.tv party over zoom with your friends. These 3 activities are crucial to help us want to keep living during these crucial times. Right now, my activity is video games #gamergirl but it's different for everyone.

SUN	MON	TUE	WED	THU	FRI	SAT
		Dance class with Maddie			Jackbox w/ LA friends	Basketball w/Ezra & friends

Pro-tip:
Each weekly schedule will include helpful hacks to reclaim you center in moments of fear and anxiety so that you are ready to face any challenge head on.

Daily Plan

What day is it? *Monday*
(Purpose: Writing down what day it is will kinesthetically help you to remember)

(To help refresh your mind and start the day with wisdom, here are some inspiring and motivational quotes that I have found to help me keep moving forward regardless of how challenging the day may seem.)

> *I can't go back to yesterday,*
> *because I was a different person then.*
> *- Alice in Wonderland*

List 3 things you are grateful for...

- Toilet paper
- My apartment
- A working phone

List 3-10 tasks you must accomplish today...

- Write an episode
- Pay rent
- Call my mother
- Set a producer meeting for TV show budget
- Book Travel for Vegas
- Check with Rich on Contract
- Cancel date politely
- Laundry

Schedule your meal times...

9:00am~9:45am	•	breakfast
11:30am~12:30pm	•	coffee break
1:00pm~2:15pm	•	Lunch
5:00pm~5:30pm	•	Snack
8:00pm~9:00pm	•	dinner

Find 2 hours for metaphysics/ belief system development

7:00am~8:00am	•	Chant
8:00am~8:10am	•	Morning meeting
8:15am~9:00am	•	Read Gosho & New Human Revolution4
: ~ :	•	
: ~ :	•	

Who do you appreciate today?
Ezra Kyle Dimalen for being one of my best friends and being there when I'm feeling low.

> *Don't think. Just do.*
> *- Anonymous*

Schedule Workouts

Example:

1. 10 Minutes of Cardio

What warmup cardio do you want to do today? (I.e. Run/Bike/Jumping Jacks)

Run

2. 10 Minute Stretch

What stretch do you want to do to-day?

Refer to YouTube video

3. 25 Minute Activity

What Activity do you want to do today? (I.e. Longboard/Long-Distance Run/Box/Dance)

Madeline's dance class

Schedule Work Time

When are your meetings for today?

10:00am~11:00am	• Book travel
2:30pm~3:30pm	• Contract w/ Rich
4:00pm~5:00pm	• Show budget w/ producers
: ~ :	•

Carry over tasks…
What couldn't you get done today? Let's carry it over into tomorrow.

I.e. Laundry

Overview
What does today look like?

7:00am~8:00am	• Chant
8:00am~8:10am	• Morning meeting
8:15am~9:00am	• Read Gosho & New Human Revolution 4
10:00am~11:00am	• Book travel & cancel date politely
11:30am~12:30pm	• Coffee break
12:00pm~12:45pm	• Workout
1:00pm~2:15pm	• Lunch
2:30pm~3:30pm	• Contract w/ Rich
4:00pm~5:00pm	• Show budget w/ producers
5:00pm~5:30pm	• Snack
5:30pm~ :	• Call mom
6:00pm~ :	• Pay rent
6:15pm~8:00pm	•
8:00pm~9:00pm	• Dinner with Ian
: ~ :	

Author's Encouragement Note

People are people. Struggles are relative to the individual. We all reach our worst and best and how we go about navigating our ways through those times are relatable. We all want to be happy and no one wants to suffer. We all have families of some kind and with that comes different challenges. We all have measures of victories and we all have measures of failures. The question remains, can we forgive ourselves for being human? Can we celebrate ourselves for achieving what we have worked hard for? Are we happy or are we suffering? At the end of the day, it's how we feel that matters most.

Regardless of all the turmoil and intensity we may have faced, look at all that we can achieve.

You are as powerful as you want to be and as great as you want to be. I'm so proud of you for taking the first step to achieve your goals and I believe in you. I'm excited to see how your dreams unfold from here!

MONTH:

_____

	SUN	MON	TUE

WED	THU	FRI	SAT

Weekly Plan

> *I don't know where I'm going from here but*
> *I promise it won't be boring.*
> *- Unknown*

1. 45-Minute Daily conditioning workouts to keep you feeling strong
True strength comes from your ability to decide and commit. The physical
conditioning is what provides practice and the refinement of your inner
strength.

SUN	MON	TUE	WED	THU	FRI	SAT

**2. Plan 3 calls each day to feel connected and mitigate the risk of isolation
& depression**
A simple "how are you doing?" or "Hey! Letting you know I'm alive" starts the
conversation and starts a connection. We are not alone and we can break
through feelings of loneliness by caring for others.

SUN	MON	TUE	WED	THU	FRI	SAT

3. Plan 3 activities a week for fun
We can't just keep working. We need to have moments of joy to be good to
ourselves and in turn good to everyone we are connected to. Schedule a dance
class or a jackbox.tv party over zoom with your friends. These 3 activities are
crucial to help us want to keep living during these times.

SUN	MON	TUE	WED	THU	FRI	SAT

Pro-tip:

Before taking a risk, (I.e. Ask someone out on a date, try a new sport, go
on an interview, etc.) listen to your favorite song and then take the
chance. Take some time to raise your vibration and be the best you. The
odds will forever be in your favor.

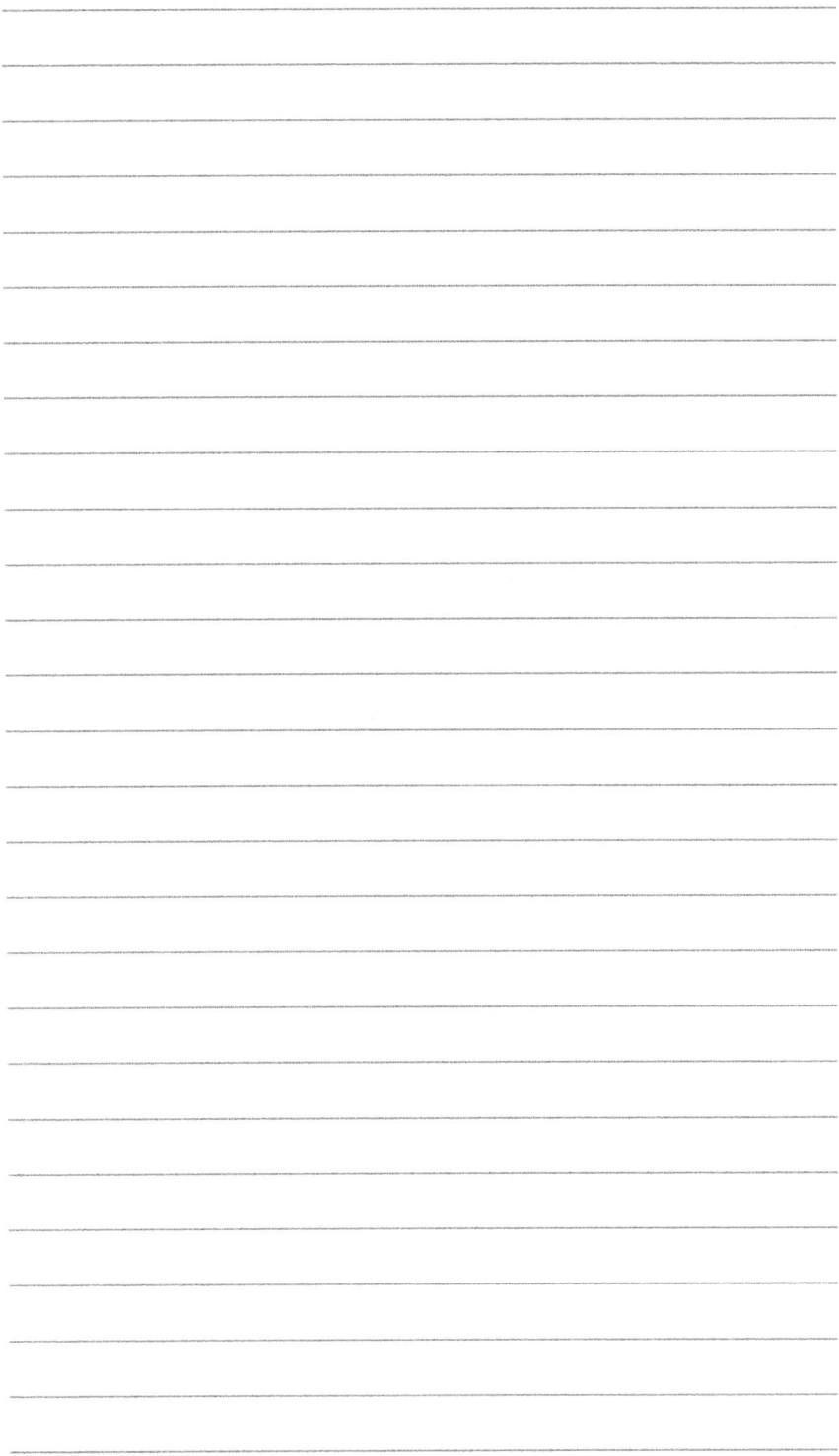

What day is it? _____

> All great masters are chiefly distinguished by the power of adding a second, a third,
> and perhaps a fourth step in a continuous line. Many a man had taken the first step.
> With every additional step, you enhance immensely the value of your first.
> – Ralph Waldo Emerson

List 3 things you are
grateful for...

- _____
- _____
- _____

List 3-10 tasks you must
accomplish today...

- _____
- _____
- _____
- _____
- _____
- _____
- _____
- _____
- _____
- _____

Schedule your meal times...

:   ~   :   •   _____
:   ~   :   •   _____
:   ~   :   •   _____
:   ~   :   •   _____
:   ~   :   •   _____

Find 2 hours for metaphysics / belief
system development...

:   ~   :   •   _____
:   ~   :   •   _____
:   ~   :   •   _____
:   ~   :   •   _____
:   ~   :   •   _____
:   ~   :   •   _____

Who do you appreciate today?

> *Make your optimism come true.*
> *– Unknown*

Schedule workouts...

1. 10-minute Cardio

_____

2. 10-minute Stretch

_____

3. 25-minute Activity

_____

Schedule work time...

When are your meetings for today?

: ~ : •

: ~ : •

: ~ : •

: ~ : •

: ~ : •

Carry over tasks...

Overview
What does today look like?

: ~ : _____

: ~ : _____

: ~ : _____

: ~ : _____

: ~ : _____

: ~ : _____

: ~ : _____

: ~ : _____

: ~ : _____

: ~ : _____

: ~ : _____

: ~ : _____

: ~ : _____

What day is it?

> *Always honor the people who opened the door to lessons.*
> *– Ace Doligosa*

List 3 things you are grateful for...

- _____
- _____
- _____

List 3-10 tasks you must accomplish today...

- _____
- _____
- _____
- _____
- _____
- _____
- _____
- _____
- _____
- _____

Schedule your meal times...

- : ~ : •
- : ~ : •
- : ~ : •
- : ~ : •
- : ~ : •

Find 2 hours for metaphysics / belief system development...

- : ~ : •
- : ~ : •
- : ~ : •
- : ~ : •
- : ~ : •
- : ~ : •

Who do you appreciate today?

> *True forgiveness is when you can say,*
> *"Thank you for that experience."*
> *– Oprah Winfrey*

Schedule workouts...

1. 10-minute Cardio

_____

2. 10-minute Stretch

_____

3. 25-minute Activity

_____

Schedule work time...

When are your meetings for today?

: ~ : •

: ~ : • _____

: ~ : • _____

: ~ : • _____

: ~ : •

Carry over tasks...

Overview
What does today look like?

: ~ : _____

: ~ : _____

: ~ : _____

: ~ : _____

: ~ : _____

: ~ : _____

: ~ : _____

: ~ : _____

: ~ : _____

: ~ : _____

: ~ : _____

: ~ : _____

What day is it?

> *It is curious that physical courage should be so common in the world and moral courage so rare.*
> *– Mark Twain*

List 3 things you are grateful for...

- _____
- _____
- _____

List 3-10 tasks you must accomplish today...

- _____
- _____
- _____
- _____
- _____
- _____
- _____
- _____
- _____
- _____

Schedule your meal times...

:   ~   :   • _____

:   ~   :   • _____

:   ~   :   • _____

:   ~   :   • _____

:   ~   :   • _____

Find 2 hours for metaphysics / belief system development...

:   ~   :   • _____

:   ~   :   • _____

:   ~   :   • _____

:   ~   :   • _____

:   ~   :   • _____

:   ~   :   • _____

Who do you appreciate today?

> *Truth is so rare that it is delightful to tell it.*
> *– Emily Dickenson*

Schedule workouts...

1. 10-minute Cardio

_____

2. 10-minute Stretch

_____

3. 25-minute Activity

_____

Schedule work time...

When are your meetings for today?

: ~ : •
_____
: ~ : •
_____
: ~ : •
_____
: ~ : •
_____
: ~ : •

Carry over tasks...

Overview
What does today look like?

: ~ : _____
: ~ : _____
: ~ : _____
: ~ : _____
: ~ : _____
: ~ : _____
: ~ : _____
: ~ : _____
: ~ : _____
: ~ : _____
: ~ : _____
: ~ : _____

What day is it? _____

> *Success is going from failure to failure*
> *without losing your enthusiasm.*
> *– Winston Churchill*

List 3 things you are
grateful for...

- _____
- _____
- _____

List 3-10 tasks you must
accomplish today...

- _____
- _____
- _____
- _____
- _____
- _____
- _____
- _____
- _____
- _____

Schedule your meal times...

: ~ : •
: ~ : •
: ~ : •
: ~ : •
: ~ : •

Find 2 hours for metaphysics / belief
system development...

: ~ : •
: ~ : •
: ~ : •
: ~ : •
: ~ : •
: ~ : •

Who do you appreciate today?

> *Enjoy when you can and endure when you must.*
> *– Johann Wolfgang von Goethe*

Schedule workouts...

1. 10-minute Cardio

_____

2. 10-minute Stretch

_____

3. 25-minute Activity

_____

Schedule work time...

When are your meetings for today?

```
:  ~  :   •  _____
:  ~  :   •  _____
:  ~  :   •  _____
:  ~  :   •  _____
:  ~  :   •  _____
```

Carry over tasks...

Overview
What does today look like?

```
:  ~  :   _____
:  ~  :   _____
:  ~  :   _____
:  ~  :   _____
:  ~  :   _____
:  ~  :   _____
:  ~  :   _____
:  ~  :   _____
:  ~  :   _____
:  ~  :   _____
:  ~  :   _____
:  ~  :   _____
```

What day is it?

> *If you are too busy to laugh, you are too busy.*
> *- Proverb*

List 3 things you are grateful for...

- _____
- _____
- _____

List 3-10 tasks you must accomplish today...

- _____
- _____
- _____
- _____
- _____
- _____
- _____
- _____
- _____
- _____

Schedule your meal times...

- ____ : ____ ~ ____ : ____ • _____
- ____ : ____ ~ ____ : ____ • _____
- ____ : ____ ~ ____ : ____ • _____
- ____ : ____ ~ ____ : ____ • _____
- ____ : ____ ~ ____ : ____ • _____

Find 2 hours for metaphysics / belief system development...

- ____ : ____ ~ ____ : ____ • _____
- ____ : ____ ~ ____ : ____ • _____
- ____ : ____ ~ ____ : ____ • _____
- ____ : ____ ~ ____ : ____ • _____
- ____ : ____ ~ ____ : ____ • _____
- ____ : ____ ~ ____ : ____ • _____

Who do you appreciate today?

> *Reflect upon your present blessings of which every man has many, not on your past misfortunes of which all men have some.*
> *— Charles Dickens*

Schedule workouts...

1. 10-minute Cardio

_____

2. 10-minute Stretch

_____

3. 25-minute Activity

_____

Schedule work time...

When are your meetings for today?

: ~ : •

_____

: ~ : •

_____

: ~ : •

_____

: ~ : •

_____

: ~ : •

Carry over tasks...

Overview
What does today look like?

: ~ : _____

: ~ : _____

: ~ : _____

: ~ : _____

: ~ : _____

: ~ : _____

: ~ : _____

: ~ : _____

: ~ : _____

: ~ : _____

: ~ : _____

: ~ : _____

What day is it?

> *Keep your face to the sunshine and*
> *you can never see the shadow.*
> *– Helen Keller*

List 3 things you are
grateful for...

- _____
- _____
- _____

List 3-10 tasks you must
accomplish today...

- _____
- _____
- _____
- _____
- _____
- _____
- _____
- _____
- _____
- _____

Schedule your meal times...

:   ~   :   • _____

:   ~   :   • _____

:   ~   :   • _____

:   ~   :   • _____

:   ~   :   • _____

Find 2 hours for metaphysics / belief
system development...

:   ~   :   • _____

:   ~   :   • _____

:   ~   :   • _____

:   ~   :   • _____

:   ~   :   • _____

:   ~   :   • _____

Who do you appreciate today?

> *It does not matter how slowly you go as long as you do not stop.*
> *- Confucius*

Schedule workouts...

1. 10-minute Cardio

_____

2. 10-minute Stretch

_____

3. 25-minute Activity

_____

Schedule work time...

When are your meetings for today?

: ~ : •
: ~ : •
: ~ : •
: ~ : •
: ~ : •

Carry over tasks...

Overview
What does today look like?

: ~ : _____
: ~ : _____
: ~ : _____
: ~ : _____
: ~ : _____
: ~ : _____
: ~ : _____
: ~ : _____
: ~ : _____
: ~ : _____
: ~ : _____
: ~ : _____
: ~ : _____

What day is it?

List 3 things you are grateful for...

- _____
- _____
- _____

List 3-10 tasks you must accomplish today...

- _____
- _____
- _____
- _____
- _____
- _____
- _____
- _____
- _____
- _____

Schedule your meal times...

: ~ : •
: ~ : • _____
: ~ : • _____
: ~ : • _____
: ~ : • _____

Find 2 hours for metaphysics / belief system development...

: ~ : • _____
: ~ : • _____
: ~ : • _____
: ~ : • _____
: ~ : • _____
: ~ : • _____

Who do you appreciate today?

> *There is no passion to be found playing small - in settling for a life that is less than the one you are capable of.*
> *— Nelson Mandela*

Schedule workouts...

1. 10-minute Cardio

_____

2. 10-minute Stretch

_____

3. 25-minute Activity

_____

Schedule work time...

When are your meetings for today?

: ~ : •

: ~ : •

: ~ : •

: ~ : •

: ~ : •

Carry over tasks...

Overview
What does today look like?

: ~ :

: ~ :

: ~ :

: ~ :

: ~ :

: ~ :

: ~ :

: ~ :

: ~ :

: ~ :

: ~ :

: ~ :

> *It is not enough just to live but that we must live well.*
> *- Socrates*

1. 45-Minute Daily conditioning workouts to keep you feeling sharp

Move a muscle. Change a thought. Train your body and you will train your mind.

SUN	MON	TUE	WED	THU	FRI	SAT

2. Plan 3 calls a day to sustain your relationships

Reach out to a friend and ask them what they have been up to. When you're circle grows, so do you.

SUN	MON	TUE	WED	THU	FRI	SAT

3. Plan 3 activities a week for fun

Try something you haven't tried before and see how your life expands.

SUN	MON	TUE	WED	THU	FRI	SAT

Pro-tip: "The 5/4/3/2/1 Rule'"
Stop what you're doing and do this now:
* Name 5 things you can see
* Name 4 things you can touch
* Name 3 things you can taste
* Name 2 things you can smell
* Name 1 thing you are grateful for

Gratitude should not be taken for granted. Trust in what or who you are grateful for and trust they will have your back. I promise you, if you keep this trust using these thoughts of gratitude, you will never be lonely again.

What day is it?

List 3 things you are grateful for...

- _____
- _____
- _____

List 3-10 tasks you must accomplish today...

- _____
- _____
- _____
- _____
- _____
- _____
- _____
- _____
- _____
- _____

Schedule your meal times...

:   ~   :   •

:   ~   :   •

:   ~   :   •

:   ~   :   •

:   ~   :   •

Find 2 hours for metaphysics / belief system development...

:   ~   :   •

:   ~   :   •

:   ~   :   •

:   ~   :   •

:   ~   :   •

:   ~   :   •

Who do you appreciate today?

> *Passion is energy. Feel the power that comes from focusing on what excites you.*
> *— Oprah Winfrey*

Schedule workouts...

1. 10-minute Cardio

_____

2. 10-minute Stretch

_____

3. 25-minute Activity

_____

Schedule work time...

When are your meetings for today?

: ~ : •

: ~ : • _____

: ~ : • _____

: ~ : • _____

: ~ : •

Carry over tasks...

Overview
What does today look like?

: ~ : _____

: ~ : _____

: ~ : _____

: ~ : _____

: ~ : _____

: ~ : _____

: ~ : _____

: ~ : _____

: ~ : _____

: ~ : _____

: ~ : _____

: ~ : _____

What day is it? ....

> *Better to take many small steps in the right direction than to
> make a great leap forward only to stumble backward.*
> *– Chinese Proverb*

List 3 things you are
grateful for...

- _____
- _____
- _____

List 3-10 tasks you must
accomplish today...

- _____
- _____
- _____
- _____
- _____
- _____
- _____
- _____
- _____
- _____

Schedule your meal times...

:	~	:	•
:	~	:	•
:	~	:	•
:	~	:	•
:	~	:	•

Find 2 hours for metaphysics / belief
system development...

:	~	:	•
:	~	:	•
:	~	:	•
:	~	:	•
:	~	:	•
:	~	:	•

Who do you appreciate today?

> *Inside every large problem is a small problem struggling to get out.*
> *– Sir Charles Antony Richard Hoare*

Schedule workouts...

1. 10-minute Cardio

_____

2. 10-minute Stretch

_____

3. 25-minute Activity

_____

Schedule work time...

When are your meetings for today?

```
:   ~   :     •  _____
:   ~   :     •  _____
:   ~   :     •  _____
:   ~   :     •  _____
:   ~   :     •  _____
```

Carry over tasks...

Overview
What does today look like?

```
:   ~   :  _____
           _____
:   ~   :  _____
           _____
:   ~   :  _____
           _____
:   ~   :  _____
           _____
:   ~   :  _____
           _____
:   ~   :  _____
           _____
:   ~   :  _____
           _____
:   ~   :  _____
           _____
:   ~   :  _____
           _____
:   ~   :  _____
           _____
:   ~   :  _____
           _____
:   ~   :  _____
           _____
```

What day is it?

> *To be wronged is nothing unless you continue to remember it.*
> *– Confucius*

List 3 things you are grateful for...

- _____
- _____
- _____

List 3-10 tasks you must accomplish today...

- _____
- _____
- _____
- _____
- _____
- _____
- _____
- _____
- _____
- _____

Schedule your meal times...

-   : ~ :   _____
-   : ~ :   _____
-   : ~ :   _____
-   : ~ :   _____
-   : ~ :   _____

Find 2 hours for metaphysics / belief system development...

-   : ~ :   _____
-   : ~ :   _____
-   : ~ :   _____
-   : ~ :   _____
-   : ~ :   _____
-   : ~ :   _____

Who do you appreciate today?

> *Being happy is the goal but greatness is my vision.*
> *– Donald Glover*

Schedule workouts...

1. 10-minute Cardio

_____

2. 10-minute Stretch

_____

3. 25-minute Activity

_____

Schedule work time...

When are your meetings for today?

: ~ : •

: ~ : •

: ~ : •

: ~ : •

: ~ : •

Carry over tasks...

Overview
What does today look like?

: ~ : _____

: ~ : _____

: ~ : _____

: ~ : _____

: ~ : _____

: ~ : _____

: ~ : _____

: ~ : _____

: ~ : _____

: ~ : _____

: ~ : _____

: ~ : _____

: ~ : _____

What day is it?

> *Get busy living or get busy dying.*
> *- Stephen King*

List 3 things you are grateful for...

- _____
- _____
- _____

List 3-10 tasks you must accomplish today...

- _____
- _____
- _____
- _____
- _____
- _____
- _____
- _____
- _____
- _____

Schedule your meal times...

- ___ : ___ ~ ___ : ___
- ___ : ___ ~ ___ : ___
- ___ : ___ ~ ___ : ___
- ___ : ___ ~ ___ : ___
- ___ : ___ ~ ___ : ___

Find 2 hours for metaphysics / belief system development...

- ___ : ___ ~ ___ : ___
- ___ : ___ ~ ___ : ___
- ___ : ___ ~ ___ : ___
- ___ : ___ ~ ___ : ___
- ___ : ___ ~ ___ : ___
- ___ : ___ ~ ___ : ___

Who do you appreciate today?

> *Yes, in all my research, the greatest leaders looked inward and were able to tell a good story with authenticity and passion.*
> *— Deepak Chopra*

Schedule workouts...

1. 10-minute Cardio

_____

2. 10-minute Stretch

_____

3. 25-minute Activity

_____

Schedule work time...

When are your meetings for today?

:   ~   :   •

:   ~   :   •   _____

:   ~   :   •   _____

:   ~   :   •   _____

:   ~   :   •

Carry over tasks...

Overview
What does today look like?

:   ~   :   _____

:   ~   :   _____

:   ~   :   _____

:   ~   :   _____

:   ~   :   _____

:   ~   :   _____

:   ~   :   _____

:   ~   :   _____

:   ~   :   _____

:   ~   :   _____

:   ~   :   _____

:   ~   :   _____

What day is it?

> *You can't fall if you don't climb. But there's no joy in living your whole life on the ground.*
> *– Unknown*

List 3 things you are grateful for...

- _____
- _____
- _____

List 3-10 tasks you must accomplish today...

- _____
- _____
- _____
- _____
- _____
- _____
- _____
- _____
- _____
- _____

Schedule your meal times...

: ~ : •

: ~ : •

: ~ : •

: ~ : •

: ~ : •

Find 2 hours for metaphysics / belief system development...

: ~ : •

: ~ : •

: ~ : •

: ~ : •

: ~ : •

: ~ : •

Who do you appreciate today?

> *In three words I can sum up everything*
> *I've learned about life: it goes on.*
> *– Robert Frost*

Schedule workouts...

1. 10-minute Cardio

_____

2. 10-minute Stretch

_____

3. 25-minute Activity

_____

Schedule work time...

When are your meetings for today?

: ~ : •
: ~ : •
: ~ : •
: ~ : •
: ~ : •

Carry over tasks...

Overview

What does today look like?

: ~ :
: ~ :
: ~ :
: ~ :
: ~ :
: ~ :
: ~ :
: ~ :
: ~ :
: ~ :
: ~ :
: ~ :

What day is it?

> *Simplicity is the ultimate sophistication.*
> *– Leonardo da Vinci*

List 3 things you are grateful for...

- _____
- _____
- _____

List 3-10 tasks you must accomplish today...

- _____
- _____
- _____
- _____
- _____
- _____
- _____
- _____
- _____
- _____

Schedule your meal times...

:   ~   :   • _____
:   ~   :   • _____
:   ~   :   • _____
:   ~   :   • _____
:   ~   :   • _____

Find 2 hours for metaphysics / belief system development...

:   ~   :   • _____
:   ~   :   • _____
:   ~   :   • _____
:   ~   :   • _____
:   ~   :   • _____
:   ~   :   • _____

Who do you appreciate today?

> *The smallest act of kindness is worth more*
> *than the grandest intention.*
> *– Oscar Wilde*

Schedule workouts...

1. 10-minute Cardio

_____

2. 10-minute Stretch

_____

3. 25-minute Activity

_____

Schedule work time...

When are your meetings for today?

:	~	:	•	
:	~	:	•	
:	~	:	•	
:	~	:	•	
:	~	:	•	

Carry over tasks...

Overview
What does today look like?

:	~	:	
:	~	:	
:	~	:	
:	~	:	
:	~	:	
:	~	:	
:	~	:	
:	~	:	
:	~	:	
:	~	:	
:	~	:	
:	~	:	

What day is it? _____

> *Strength does not come from physical capacity. It comes from an indomitable will.*
> *– Mahatma Gandhi*

List 3 things you are grateful for...

- _____
- _____
- _____

List 3-10 tasks you must accomplish today...

- _____
- _____
- _____
- _____
- _____
- _____
- _____
- _____
- _____
- _____

Schedule your meal times...

:   ~   :   • _____

:   ~   :   • _____

:   ~   :   • _____

:   ~   :   • _____

:   ~   :   • _____

Find 2 hours for metaphysics / belief system development...

:   ~   :   • _____

:   ~   :   • _____

:   ~   :   • _____

:   ~   :   • _____

:   ~   :   • _____

:   ~   :   • _____

Who do you appreciate today?

> *Plenty of men can do good work for a spurt with immediate promotion in mind.*
> *But for promotion, you want a good man in whom good work has become a habit.*
> *— Henry Doherty*

Schedule workouts...

1. 10-minute Cardio

_____

2. 10-minute Stretch

_____

3. 25-minute Activity

_____

Schedule work time...

When are your meetings for today?

: ~ : •
_____
: ~ : •
_____
: ~ : •
_____
: ~ : •
_____
: ~ : •

Carry over tasks...

Overview
What does today look like?

: ~ : _____
: ~ : _____
: ~ : _____
: ~ : _____
: ~ : _____
: ~ : _____
: ~ : _____
: ~ : _____
: ~ : _____
: ~ : _____
: ~ : _____
: ~ : _____
: ~ : _____

Weekly Plan

> *I don't know where I'm going from here,*
> *but I promise it won't be boring.*
> *- David Bowie*

1. 45-Minute Daily conditioning workouts to keep you feeling sharp

"Nothing like a good workout to relieve stress and refocus our minds on what's most important. I hope you all are having a great start to your week, taking care of/helping those around you and getting after it." - @scott_mathison_

SUN	MON	TUE	WED	THU	FRI	SAT

2. Plan 3 calls a day to sustain your relationships

Sometimes the best way to support your friends is to call and ask if they're doing okay. I challenge you to sit back and listen for them to finish their whole thought. Then, respond after you digest exactly what they're saying. "'Vulnerability is the key to connection because it is the courage to be open to another human being.' This courage then gives the other person permission within themselves to open up and be vulnerable as well." - @chrisjcarton

SUN	MON	TUE	WED	THU	FRI	SAT

3. Plan 3 activities a week for fun

Try something you haven't tried before and see how your life expands.

SUN	MON	TUE	WED	THU	FRI	SAT

Pro-tip:

Plan your day in 30 minutes. Practicing quick decision making will leave room for more action in your day. The quicker you can decide, the more you can do.

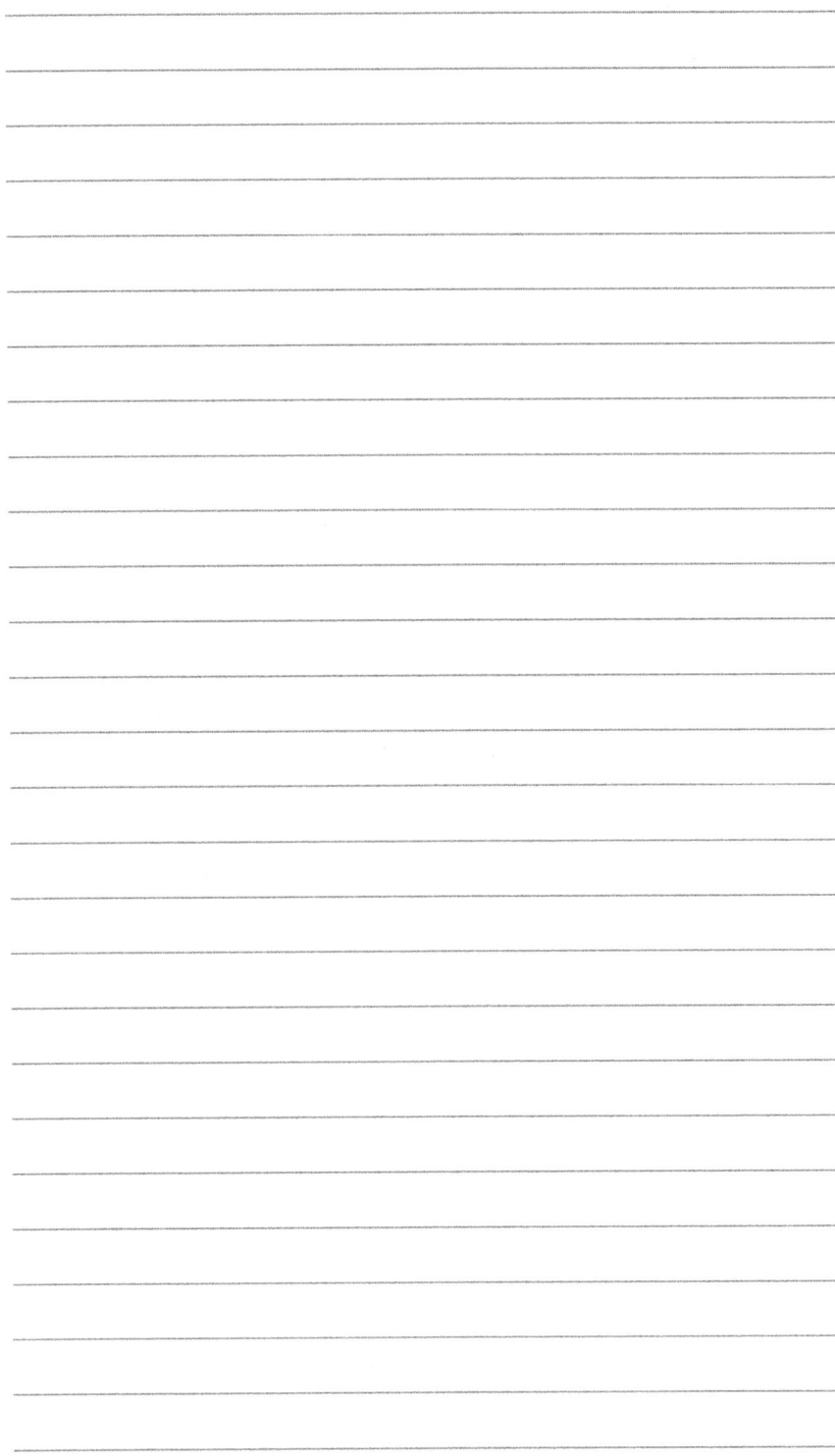

What day is it?

> *Each person will show you a different side of you.*
> *– Ace Doligosa*

List 3 things you are
grateful for...

- _____
- _____
- _____

List 3-10 tasks you must
accomplish today...

- _____
- _____
- _____
- _____
- _____
- _____
- _____
- _____
- _____
- _____

Schedule your meal times...

: ~ : •
: ~ : •
: ~ : •
: ~ : •
: ~ : •

Find 2 hours for metaphysics / belief
system development...

: ~ : •
: ~ : •
: ~ : •
: ~ : •
: ~ : •
: ~ : •

Who do you appreciate today?

> *Cultivate the habit of being grateful for every good thing that comes to you, and to give thanks continuously. And because all things have contributed to your advancement, you should include all things in your gratitude.*
> *– Ralph Waldo Emerson*

Schedule workouts...

1. 10-minute Cardio

_____

2. 10-minute Stretch

_____

3. 25-minute Activity

_____

Schedule work time...

When are your meetings for today?

: ~ : •

: ~ : •

: ~ : •

: ~ : •

: ~ : •

Carry over tasks...

Overview
What does today look like?

: ~ :

: ~ :

: ~ :

: ~ :

: ~ :

: ~ :

: ~ :

: ~ :

: ~ :

: ~ :

: ~ :

: ~ :

What day is it?

List 3 things you are grateful for...

- _____
- _____
- _____

List 3-10 tasks you must accomplish today...

- _____
- _____
- _____
- _____
- _____
- _____
- _____
- _____
- _____

Schedule your meal times...

:   ~   :   •
:   ~   :   •
:   ~   :   •
:   ~   :   •
:   ~   :   •

Find 2 hours for metaphysics / belief system development...

:   ~   :   •
:   ~   :   •
:   ~   :   •
:   ~   :   •
:   ~   :   •
:   ~   :   •

Who do you appreciate today?

> *Courage is what it takes to stand up and speak; courage is also what it takes to sit down and listen.*
> *– Winston Churchill*

Schedule workouts...

1. 10-minute Cardio

_____

2. 10-minute Stretch

_____

3. 25-minute Activity

_____

Schedule work time...

When are your meetings for today?

: ~ : •

: ~ : • _____

: ~ : • _____

: ~ : • _____

: ~ : •

Carry over tasks...

Overview
What does today look like?

: ~ : _____

: ~ : _____

: ~ : _____

: ~ : _____

: ~ : _____

: ~ : _____

: ~ : _____

: ~ : _____

: ~ : _____

: ~ : _____

: ~ : _____

: ~ : _____

What day is it? _____

List 3 things you are grateful for...

- _____
- _____
- _____

List 3-10 tasks you must accomplish today...

- _____
- _____
- _____
- _____
- _____
- _____
- _____
- _____
- _____
- _____

Schedule your meal times...

: ~ : •
: ~ : •
: ~ : •
: ~ : •
: ~ : •

Find 2 hours for metaphysics / belief system development...

: ~ : •
: ~ : •
: ~ : •
: ~ : •
: ~ : •
: ~ : •

Who do you appreciate today?

> *Logic will get you from A to B.*
> *Imagination will take you everywhere.*
> *- Albert Einstein*

Schedule workouts...

1. 10-minute Cardio

_____

2. 10-minute Stretch

_____

3. 25-minute Activity

_____

Schedule work time...

When are your meetings for today?

:   ~   :   •
:   ~   :   •
:   ~   :   •
:   ~   :   •
:   ~   :   •

Carry over tasks...

Overview
What does today look like?

:   ~   :
:   ~   :
:   ~   :
:   ~   :
:   ~   :
:   ~   :
:   ~   :
:   ~   :
:   ~   :
:   ~   :
:   ~   :
:   ~   :

What day is it?

List 3 things you are grateful for...

- _____
- _____
- _____

List 3-10 tasks you must accomplish today...

- _____
- _____
- _____
- _____
- _____
- _____
- _____
- _____
- _____
- _____

Schedule your meal times...

:   ~   :   •

:   ~   :   •

:   ~   :   •

:   ~   :   •

:   ~   :   •

Find 2 hours for metaphysics / belief system development...

:   ~   :   •

:   ~   :   •

:   ~   :   •

:   ~   :   •

:   ~   :   •

:   ~   :   •

Who do you appreciate today?

> *Only reason why people quit - is because*
> *they are focused on their current situation.*
> *- Kash Raston*

Schedule workouts...

1. 10-minute Cardio

_____

2. 10-minute Stretch

_____

3. 25-minute Activity

_____

Schedule work time...

When are your meetings for today?

: ~ : •

: ~ : •

: ~ : •

: ~ : •

: ~ : •

Carry over tasks...

Overview

What does today look like?

: ~ :

: ~ :

: ~ :

: ~ :

: ~ :

: ~ :

: ~ :

: ~ :

: ~ :

: ~ :

: ~ :

: ~ :

What day is it? ....

> *Every single person is valuable because every single person has the ability to serve.*

List 3 things you are grateful for...

- _____
- _____
- _____

List 3-10 tasks you must accomplish today...

- _____
- _____
- _____
- _____
- _____
- _____
- _____
- _____
- _____
- _____

Schedule your meal times...

- : ~ : •
- : ~ : •
- : ~ : •
- : ~ : •
- : ~ : •

Find 2 hours for metaphysics / belief system development...

- : ~ : •
- : ~ : •
- : ~ : •
- : ~ : •
- : ~ : •
- : ~ : •

Who do you appreciate today?

> *Follow your own path, no matter what people say.*
> *- Karl Marx*

Schedule workouts...

1. 10-minute Cardio

_____

2. 10-minute Stretch

_____

3. 25-minute Activity

_____

Schedule work time...

When are your meetings for today?

: ~ : •

: ~ : •

: ~ : •

: ~ : •

: ~ : •

Carry over tasks...

Overview
What does today look like?

: ~ :

: ~ :

: ~ :

: ~ :

: ~ :

: ~ :

: ~ :

: ~ :

: ~ :

: ~ :

: ~ :

: ~ :

What day is it?

List 3 things you are grateful for...

- _____
- _____
- _____

List 3-10 tasks you must accomplish today...

- _____
- _____
- _____
- _____
- _____
- _____
- _____
- _____
- _____
- _____

Schedule your meal times...

: ~ : •
: ~ : •
: ~ : •
: ~ : •
: ~ : •

Find 2 hours for metaphysics / belief system development...

: ~ : •
: ~ : •
: ~ : •
: ~ : •
: ~ : •
: ~ : •

Who do you appreciate today?

> *Mastering others is strength. Mastering oneself makes you fearless.*
> *– Lao Tzu*

Schedule workouts...

1. 10-minute Cardio

_____

2. 10-minute Stretch

_____

3. 25-minute Activity

_____

Schedule work time...

When are your meetings for today?

- : ~ : •
- : ~ : • _____
- : ~ : • _____
- : ~ : • _____
- : ~ : • _____

Carry over tasks...

Overview
What does today look like?

: ~ : _____

: ~ : _____

: ~ : _____

: ~ : _____

: ~ : _____

: ~ : _____

: ~ : _____

: ~ : _____

: ~ : _____

: ~ : _____

: ~ : _____

: ~ : _____

What day is it? ....

> *Be curious not judgmental.*
> *-Walt Whitman*

List 3 things you are
grateful for...

- _____
- _____
- _____

List 3-10 tasks you must
accomplish today...

- _____
- _____
- _____
- _____
- _____
- _____
- _____
- _____
- _____
- _____

Schedule your meal times...

- : ~ : •
- : ~ : •
- : ~ : •
- : ~ : •
- : ~ : •

Find 2 hours for metaphysics / belief
system development...

- : ~ : •
- : ~ : •
- : ~ : •
- : ~ : •
- : ~ : •
- : ~ : •

Who do you appreciate today?

> *Loyalty to a petrified opinion never broke a chain nor freed a soul.*
> *– Mark Twain*

Schedule workouts...

1. 10-minute Cardio

_____

2. 10-minute Stretch

_____

3. 25-minute Activity

_____

Schedule work time...

When are your meetings for today?

: ~ : •

: ~ : •

: ~ : •

: ~ : •

: ~ : •

Carry over tasks...

Overview
What does today look like?

: ~ : _____

: ~ : _____

: ~ : _____

: ~ : _____

: ~ : _____

: ~ : _____

: ~ : _____

: ~ : _____

: ~ : _____

: ~ : _____

: ~ : _____

: ~ : _____

: ~ : _____

Weekly Plan

1. 45-Minute Daily conditioning workouts to keep you feeling sharp

"In order to excel at anything, there are always hurdles, obstacles, or challenges one must get past. It's what bodybuilders call the pain period. Those who push themselves and are willing to face pain, exhaustion, humiliation, rejection, or worse are the ones who become champions." - Neil Strauss

SUN	MON	TUE	WED	THU	FRI	SAT

2. Plan 3 calls a day to feel grounded

Reach out to hometown friends, family friends, family members, or your parents this week. Have the courage to ask them how they are doing and the compassion to connect with them.

SUN	MON	TUE	WED	THU	FRI	SAT

3. Plan 3 activities a week for fun

Try something you haven't tried before and see how your life expands.

SUN	MON	TUE	WED	THU	FRI	SAT

Pro-tip:

Take a day to give back to the community and do some community service. First, think about what you are passionate about. From there search the places that accept volunteers. I had a passion for children and decided to volunteer at *Give Kids the World*. Here, children with critical illnesses and their families are treated to weeklong, cost-free vacations. Think about what you are happy to do for free and do it.

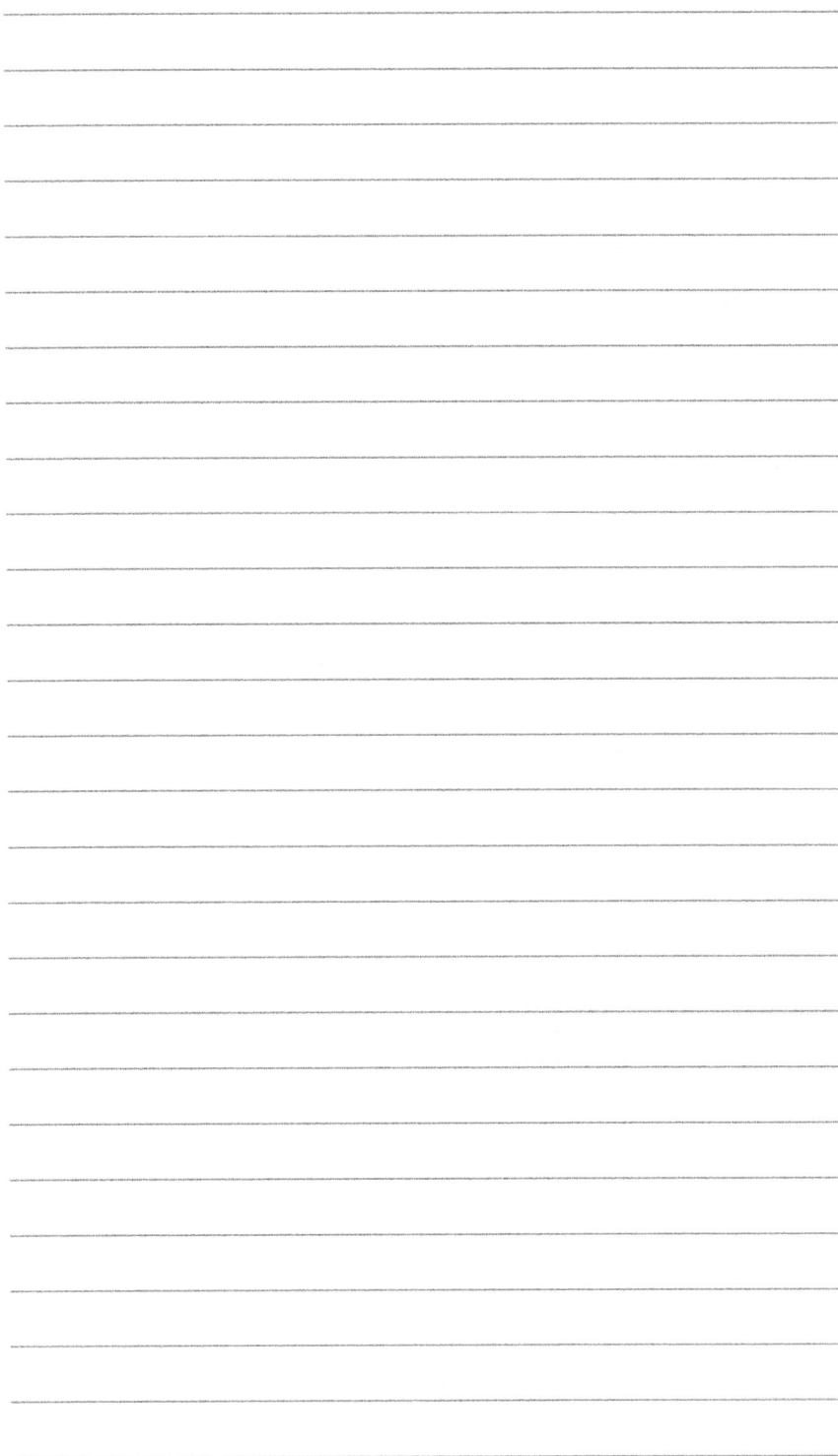

What day is it? ....

> *Where there is love, there is life.*
> *— Mahatma Gandhi*

List 3 things you are grateful for...

- _____
- _____
- _____

List 3-10 tasks you must accomplish today...

- _____
- _____
- _____
- _____
- _____
- _____
- _____
- _____
- _____
- _____

Schedule your meal times...

: ~ : •
: ~ : •
: ~ : •
: ~ : •
: ~ : •

Find 2 hours for metaphysics / belief system development...

: ~ : •
: ~ : •
: ~ : •
: ~ : •
: ~ : •
: ~ : •

Who do you appreciate today?

> *I would rather make mistakes in kindness and compassion than work miracles in unkindness and hardness.*
> *— Mother Theresa*

Schedule workouts...

1. 10-minute Cardio

_____

2. 10-minute Stretch

_____

3. 25-minute Activity

_____

Schedule work time...

When are your meetings for today?

: ~ :   • _____

: ~ :   • _____

: ~ :   • _____

: ~ :   • _____

: ~ :   • _____

Carry over tasks...

Overview
What does today look like?

: ~ :   _____

: ~ :   _____

: ~ :   _____

: ~ :   _____

: ~ :   _____

: ~ :   _____

: ~ :   _____

: ~ :   _____

: ~ :   _____

: ~ :   _____

: ~ :   _____

: ~ :   _____

: ~ :   _____

What day is it?

> *Courage is not simply one of the virtues but the form of every virtue at the testing point.*
> *– C.S. Lewis*

List 3 things you are grateful for...

- _____
- _____
- _____

List 3-10 tasks you must accomplish today...

- _____
- _____
- _____
- _____
- _____
- _____
- _____
- _____
- _____
- _____

Schedule your meal times...

- : ~ : •
- : ~ : •
- : ~ : •
- : ~ : •
- : ~ : •

Find 2 hours for metaphysics / belief system development...

- : ~ : •
- : ~ : •
- : ~ : •
- : ~ : •
- : ~ : •
- : ~ : •

Who do you appreciate today?

> *A good leader matched with a good idea is a recipe for success.*
> *- Rondil Gosine*

Schedule workouts...

1. 10-minute Cardio

_____

2. 10-minute Stretch

_____

3. 25-minute Activity

_____

Schedule work time...

When are your meetings for today?

: ~ : •

: ~ : •

: ~ : •

: ~ : •

: ~ : •

Carry over tasks...

Overview
What does today look like?

: ~ :

: ~ :

: ~ :

: ~ :

: ~ :

: ~ :

: ~ :

: ~ :

: ~ :

: ~ :

: ~ :

: ~ :

What day is it?

> *Sometimes we use our energy to hit ourselves after a mistake and then we stagnate. We really should be using that energy to propel ourselves forward.*
> *- Ace Doligosa*

List 3 things you are grateful for...

- _____
- _____
- _____

List 3-10 tasks you must accomplish today...

- _____
- _____
- _____
- _____
- _____
- _____
- _____
- _____
- _____
- _____

Schedule your meal times...

: ~ : •
: ~ : •
: ~ : •
: ~ : •
: ~ : •

Find 2 hours for metaphysics / belief system development...

: ~ : •
: ~ : •
: ~ : •
: ~ : •
: ~ : •
: ~ : •

Who do you appreciate today?

> *Listen. Empower your teams. Treat everyday like it's your first.*
> *- Steph McMahon*

Schedule workouts...

1. 10-minute Cardio

_____

2. 10-minute Stretch

_____

3. 25-minute Activity

_____

Schedule work time...

When are your meetings for today?

: ~ : •

: ~ : •

: ~ : •

: ~ : •

: ~ : •

Carry over tasks...

Overview
What does today look like?

: ~ :

: ~ :

: ~ :

: ~ :

: ~ :

: ~ :

: ~ :

: ~ :

: ~ :

: ~ :

: ~ :

: ~ :

What day is it? ....

> *It is impossible to overstate the power of free, zero dollars means zero barriers...*
> *- Linda Yaccarino*

List 3 things you are grateful for...

- _____
- _____
- _____

List 3-10 tasks you must accomplish today...

- _____
- _____
- _____
- _____
- _____
- _____
- _____
- _____
- _____
- _____

Schedule your meal times...

:	~	:	•
:	~	:	•
:	~	:	•
:	~	:	•
:	~	:	•

Find 2 hours for metaphysics / belief system development...

:	~	:	•
:	~	:	•
:	~	:	•
:	~	:	•
:	~	:	•
:	~	:	•

Who do you appreciate today?

> *The biggest mistake to me is complacency.*
> *- Bonnie Hammer*

Schedule workouts...

1. 10-minute Cardio

_____

2. 10-minute Stretch

_____

3. 25-minute Activity

_____

Schedule work time...

When are your meetings for today?

: ~ : •

: ~ : •

: ~ : •

: ~ : •

: ~ : •

Carry over tasks...

Overview
What does today look like?

: ~ :

: ~ :

: ~ :

: ~ :

: ~ :

: ~ :

: ~ :

: ~ :

: ~ :

: ~ :

: ~ :

What day is it?

> *Coming together is a beginning. Keeping together is a process. Working together is a success.*
> *– Henry Ford*

List 3 things you are grateful for...

- _____
- _____
- _____

List 3-10 tasks you must accomplish today...

- _____
- _____
- _____
- _____
- _____
- _____
- _____
- _____
- _____
- _____

Schedule your meal times...

: ~ : •
: ~ : • _____
: ~ : • _____
: ~ : • _____
: ~ : • _____

Find 2 hours for metaphysics / belief system development...

: ~ : •
: ~ : • _____
: ~ : • _____
: ~ : • _____
: ~ : • _____
: ~ : • _____

Who do you appreciate today?

> *As we look ahead into the next century, leaders will be those who empower others.*
> *– Bill Gates*

Schedule workouts...

1. 10-minute Cardio

_____

2. 10-minute Stretch

_____

3. 25-minute Activity

_____

Schedule work time...

When are your meetings for today?

: ~ : •
_____

: ~ : •
_____

: ~ : •
_____

: ~ : •
_____

: ~ : •

Carry over tasks...

Overview
What does today look like?

: ~ :
_____

: ~ :
_____

: ~ :
_____

: ~ :
_____

: ~ :
_____

: ~ :
_____

: ~ :
_____

: ~ :
_____

: ~ :
_____

: ~ :
_____

: ~ :
_____

: ~ :
_____

What day is it? ⎯⎯⎯⎯⎯⎯⎯⎯⎯⎯⎯⎯⎯

> *If you build castles in the air, your world need not be lost; that is*
> *where they should be. Now put the foundations under them.*
> *– Henry David Thoreau*

List 3 things you are
grateful for...

- ⎯⎯⎯⎯⎯⎯⎯⎯⎯
- ⎯⎯⎯⎯⎯⎯⎯⎯⎯
- ⎯⎯⎯⎯⎯⎯⎯⎯⎯

List 3-10 tasks you must
accomplish today...

- ⎯⎯⎯⎯⎯⎯⎯⎯⎯
- ⎯⎯⎯⎯⎯⎯⎯⎯⎯
- ⎯⎯⎯⎯⎯⎯⎯⎯⎯
- ⎯⎯⎯⎯⎯⎯⎯⎯⎯
- ⎯⎯⎯⎯⎯⎯⎯⎯⎯
- ⎯⎯⎯⎯⎯⎯⎯⎯⎯
- ⎯⎯⎯⎯⎯⎯⎯⎯⎯
- ⎯⎯⎯⎯⎯⎯⎯⎯⎯
- ⎯⎯⎯⎯⎯⎯⎯⎯⎯

Schedule your meal times...

```
:    ~    :    •
:    ~    :    •
:    ~    :    •
:    ~    :    •
:    ~    :    •
```

Find 2 hours for metaphysics / belief
system development...

```
:    ~    :    •
:    ~    :    •
:    ~    :    •
:    ~    :    •
:    ~    :    •
:    ~    :    •
```

Who do you appreciate today?

> *The journey of a thousand miles begins with one step.*
> *– Lao Tzu*

Schedule workouts...

1. 10-minute Cardio

_____

2. 10-minute Stretch

_____

3. 25-minute Activity

_____

Schedule work time...

When are your meetings for today?

: ~ : •
_____
: ~ : •
_____
: ~ : •
_____
: ~ : •
_____
: ~ : •

Carry over tasks...

Overview
What does today look like?

: ~ : _____
: ~ : _____
: ~ : _____
: ~ : _____
: ~ : _____
: ~ : _____
: ~ : _____
: ~ : _____
: ~ : _____
: ~ : _____
: ~ : _____
: ~ : _____
: ~ : _____

What day is it? ....

> *Stop acting so small.*
> *You are the universe in ecstatic motion.*
> *— Rumi*

List 3 things you are grateful for...

- _____
- _____
- _____

List 3-10 tasks you must accomplish today...

- _____
- _____
- _____
- _____
- _____
- _____
- _____
- _____
- _____
- _____

Schedule your meal times...

: ~ : •
: ~ : •
: ~ : •
: ~ : •
: ~ : •

Find 2 hours for metaphysics / belief system development...

: ~ : •
: ~ : •
: ~ : •
: ~ : •
: ~ : •
: ~ : •

Who do you appreciate today?

> *I work very hard and I play very hard. I'm grateful for life.
> And I live it – I believe life loves the liver of it. I live it.*
> *– Maya Angelou*

Schedule workouts…

1. 10-minute Cardio

_____

2. 10-minute Stretch

_____

3. 25-minute Activity

_____

Schedule work time…

When are your meetings for today?

: ~ : •

: ~ : •

: ~ : •

: ~ : •

: ~ : •

Carry over tasks…

Overview

What does today look like?

: ~ :

: ~ :

: ~ :

: ~ :

: ~ :

: ~ :

: ~ :

: ~ :

: ~ :

: ~ :

: ~ :

: ~ :

> *What you seek is seeking you.*
> *- Rumi*

1. 45-Minute Daily conditioning workouts to keep you feeling sharp

Move a muscle, change a thought. Train your body and you will train your mind.

SUN	MON	TUE	WED	THU	FRI	SAT

2. Plan 3 calls a day to feel grounded

Reach out to a friend and ask them what they have been up to. When your circle grows, so do you.

SUN	MON	TUE	WED	THU	FRI	SAT

3. Plan 3 activities a week for fun

Try something you haven't tried before and see how your life expands.

SUN	MON	TUE	WED	THU	FRI	SAT

Pro-tip:

People say all the time, remove your emotions from conversation - I completely disagree. There is no true conversation without feelings - acknowledge your emotions and harness them with your words. I respect anyone who has the courage to challenge what is wrong and the courage to appreciate what is right.

What day is it? _____

> *Where ever you go, go with all your heart.*
> *— Confucius*

List 3 things you are
grateful for...

- _____
- _____
- _____

Schedule your meal times...

:   ~   :   •
:   ~   :   •
:   ~   :   •
:   ~   :   •
:   ~   :   •

List 3-10 tasks you must
accomplish today...

- _____
- _____
- _____
- _____
- _____
- _____
- _____
- _____
- _____
- _____

Find 2 hours for metaphysics / belief
system development...

:   ~   :   •
:   ~   :   •
:   ~   :   •
:   ~   :   •
:   ~   :   •

Who do you appreciate today?

> *Remembering that you are going to die is the best way I know to avoid the trap of thinking you have something to lose. You are already naked. There is no reason not to follow your heart.*
> *– Steve Jobs*

Schedule workouts...

1. 10-minute Cardio

_____

2. 10-minute Stretch

_____

3. 25-minute Activity

_____

Schedule work time...

When are your meetings for today?

```
: ~ :  •
: ~ :  •
: ~ :  •
: ~ :  •
: ~ :  •
```

Carry over tasks...

Overview
What does today look like?

```
: ~ :
: ~ :
: ~ :
: ~ :
: ~ :
: ~ :
: ~ :
: ~ :
: ~ :
: ~ :
: ~ :
: ~ :
```

What day is it?

> *Great things never come from comfort zones.*
> *– Unknown*

List 3 things you are grateful for...

- _____
- _____
- _____

List 3-10 tasks you must accomplish today...

- _____
- _____
- _____
- _____
- _____
- _____
- _____
- _____
- _____
- _____

Schedule your meal times...

- : ~ : •
- : ~ : •
- : ~ : •
- : ~ : •
- : ~ : •

Find 2 hours for metaphysics / belief system development...

- : ~ : •
- : ~ : •
- : ~ : •
- : ~ : •
- : ~ : •
- : ~ : •

Who do you appreciate today?

> *The greatest revenge is massive success.*
> *– Les Brown*

Schedule workouts...

1. 10-minute Cardio

_____

2. 10-minute Stretch

_____

3. 25-minute Activity

_____

Schedule work time...

When are your meetings for today?

: ~ : •

: ~ : • _____

: ~ : • _____

: ~ : • _____

: ~ : •

Carry over tasks...

Overview
What does today look like?

: ~ : _____

: ~ : _____

: ~ : _____

: ~ : _____

: ~ : _____

: ~ : _____

: ~ : _____

: ~ : _____

: ~ : _____

: ~ : _____

: ~ : _____

: ~ : _____

What day is it?

> *Whatever you want in life, other people are going to want it too.*
> *Believe in yourself enough to accept the idea that you have an equal*
> *right to it.*
> *- Diane Sawyer*

List 3 things you are
grateful for...

- _____
- _____
- _____

List 3-10 tasks you must
accomplish today...

- _____
- _____
- _____
- _____
- _____
- _____
- _____
- _____
- _____
- _____

Schedule your meal times...

: ~ : •
: ~ : • _____
: ~ : • _____
: ~ : • _____
: ~ : • _____

Find 2 hours for metaphysics / belief
system development...

: ~ : •
: ~ : • _____
: ~ : • _____
: ~ : • _____
: ~ : • _____
: ~ : • _____

Who do you appreciate today?

> *Define success on your own terms, achieve it by your own rules, and build a life you're proud to live.*
> *- Anne Sweeney*

Schedule workouts...

1. 10-minute Cardio

_____

2. 10-minute Stretch

_____

3. 25-minute Activity

_____

Schedule work time...

When are your meetings for today?

: ' ~ : •
_____
: ~ : •
_____
: ~ : •
_____
: ~ : •
_____
: ~ : •

Carry over tasks...

Overview
What does today look like?

: ~ : _____
: ~ : _____
: ~ : _____
: ~ : _____
: ~ : _____
: ~ : _____
: ~ : _____
: ~ : _____
: ~ : _____
: ~ : _____
: ~ : _____
: ~ : _____

What day is it?

> *Life shrinks or expands in proportion to one's courage.*
> *- Anais Nin*

List 3 things you are grateful for...

- _____
- _____
- _____

List 3-10 tasks you must accomplish today...

- _____
- _____
- _____
- _____
- _____
- _____
- _____
- _____
- _____
- _____

Schedule your meal times...

: ~ : •
: ~ : •
: ~ : •
: ~ : •
: ~ : •

Find 2 hours for metaphysics / belief system development...

: ~ : •
: ~ : •
: ~ : •
: ~ : •
: ~ : •
: ~ : •

Who do you appreciate today?

> *To handle yourself, use your head; to handle others, use your heart.*
> *- Eleanor Roosevelt*

Schedule workouts...

1. 10-minute Cardio

_____

2. 10-minute Stretch

_____

3. 25-minute Activity

_____

Schedule work time...

When are your meetings for today?

:   ~   :   •

:   ~   :   •   _____

:   ~   :   •   _____

:   ~   :   •   _____

:   ~   :   •

Carry over tasks...

Overview
What does today look like?

:   ~   :   _____

:   ~   :   _____

:   ~   :   _____

:   ~   :   _____

:   ~   :   _____

:   ~   :   _____

:   ~   :   _____

:   ~   :   _____

:   ~   :   _____

:   ~   :   _____

:   ~   :   _____

What day is it? ....

> *Done is better than perfect.*
> *- Sheryl Sandberg*

List 3 things you are grateful for...

- _____
- _____
- _____

List 3-10 tasks you must accomplish today...

- _____
- _____
- _____
- _____
- _____
- _____
- _____
- _____
- _____
- _____

Schedule your meal times...

  :   ~   :   •
  :   ~   :   •
  :   ~   :   •
  :   ~   :   •
  :   ~   :   •

Find 2 hours for metaphysics / belief system development...

  :   ~   :   •
  :   ~   :   •
  :   ~   :   •
  :   ~   :   •
  :   ~   :   •

Who do you appreciate today?

> *You get in life what you have the courage to ask for.*
> *-Nancy D. Solomon*

Schedule workouts...

1. 10-minute Cardio

_____

2. 10-minute Stretch

_____

3. 25-minute Activity

_____

Schedule work time...

When are your meetings for today?

```
:   ~   :   •
:   ~   :   •
:   ~   :   •
:   ~   :   •
:   ~   :   •
```

Carry over tasks...

Overview
What does today look like?

```
:   ~   :
:   ~   :
:   ~   :
:   ~   :
:   ~   :
:   ~   :
:   ~   :
:   ~   :
:   ~   :
:   ~   :
:   ~   :
:   ~   :
```

What day is it?

List 3 things you are grateful for...

- _____
- _____
- _____

List 3-10 tasks you must accomplish today...

- _____
- _____
- _____
- _____
- _____
- _____
- _____
- _____
- _____
- _____

Schedule your meal times...

:   ~   :   •
:   ~   :   •
:   ~   :   •
:   ~   :   •
:   ~   :   •

Find 2 hours for metaphysics / belief system development...

:   ~   :   •
:   ~   :   •
:   ~   :   •
:   ~   :   •
:   ~   :   •
:   ~   :   •

Who do you appreciate today?

> *If your dream only includes you, it's too small.*
> *- Ava DuVernay*

Schedule workouts...

1. 10-minute Cardio

_____

2. 10-minute Stretch

_____

3. 25-minute Activity

_____

Schedule work time...

When are your meetings for today?

: ~ : •
_____

: ~ : •
_____

: ~ : •
_____

: ~ : •
_____

: ~ : •

Carry over tasks...

Overview
What does today look like?

: ~ :
_____

: ~ :
_____

: ~ :
_____

: ~ :
_____

: ~ :
_____

: ~ :
_____

: ~ :
_____

: ~ :
_____

: ~ :
_____

: ~ :
_____

: ~ :
_____

: ~ :
_____

What day is it?

> *The mark of a great man is one who knows when to set aside the important things in order to accomplish the vital ones.*
> *- Brandon Sanderson*

List 3 things you are grateful for...

- _____
- _____
- _____

List 3-10 tasks you must accomplish today...

- _____
- _____
- _____
- _____
- _____
- _____
- _____
- _____
- _____
- _____

Schedule your meal times...

: ~ : •
: ~ : •
: ~ : •
: ~ : •
: ~ : •

Find 2 hours for metaphysics / belief system development...

: ~ : •
: ~ : •
: ~ : •
: ~ : •
: ~ : •
: ~ : •
: ~ : •

Who do you appreciate today?

> *Being a great leader means sometimes pissing people off.*
> *- Colin Powell*

Schedule workouts...

1. 10-minute Cardio

_____

2. 10-minute Stretch

_____

3. 25-minute Activity

_____

Schedule work time...

When are your meetings for today?

```
:   ~   :   •
_____
:   ~   :   •
_____
:   ~   :   •
_____
:   ~   :   •
_____
:   ~   :   •
```

Carry over tasks...

Overview
What does today look like?

```
:   ~   :   _____
:   ~   :   _____
:   ~   :   _____
:   ~   :   _____
:   ~   :   _____
:   ~   :   _____
:   ~   :   _____
:   ~   :   _____
:   ~   :   _____
:   ~   :   _____
:   ~   :   _____
:   ~   :   _____
```

Vision and Goals

What is your definition of success?

When you have made it, who is by your side?

What are the newspapers saying about your success story?

What does it feel like?

Where are you living?

Who have you paid back?

What promises have you kept?

Who have you made proud?

Describe the following parts of your life

Relationships / Social

Career

Finances

Love

Home life

Recreational / Hobbies

Why do you deserve your dream (What impact will you make while you are achieving your dream?)

Name 5 reasons:

     1.

     2.

     3.

     4.

     5.

Are my current behaviors and habits aligned with my life vision?

What are the milestones to get there?

What are your 3-year goals towards this dream?

Think bigger...

What are your 5-year goals towards this dream?

What are your 10-year goals towards this dream?

What are your 30-year goals towards this dream?

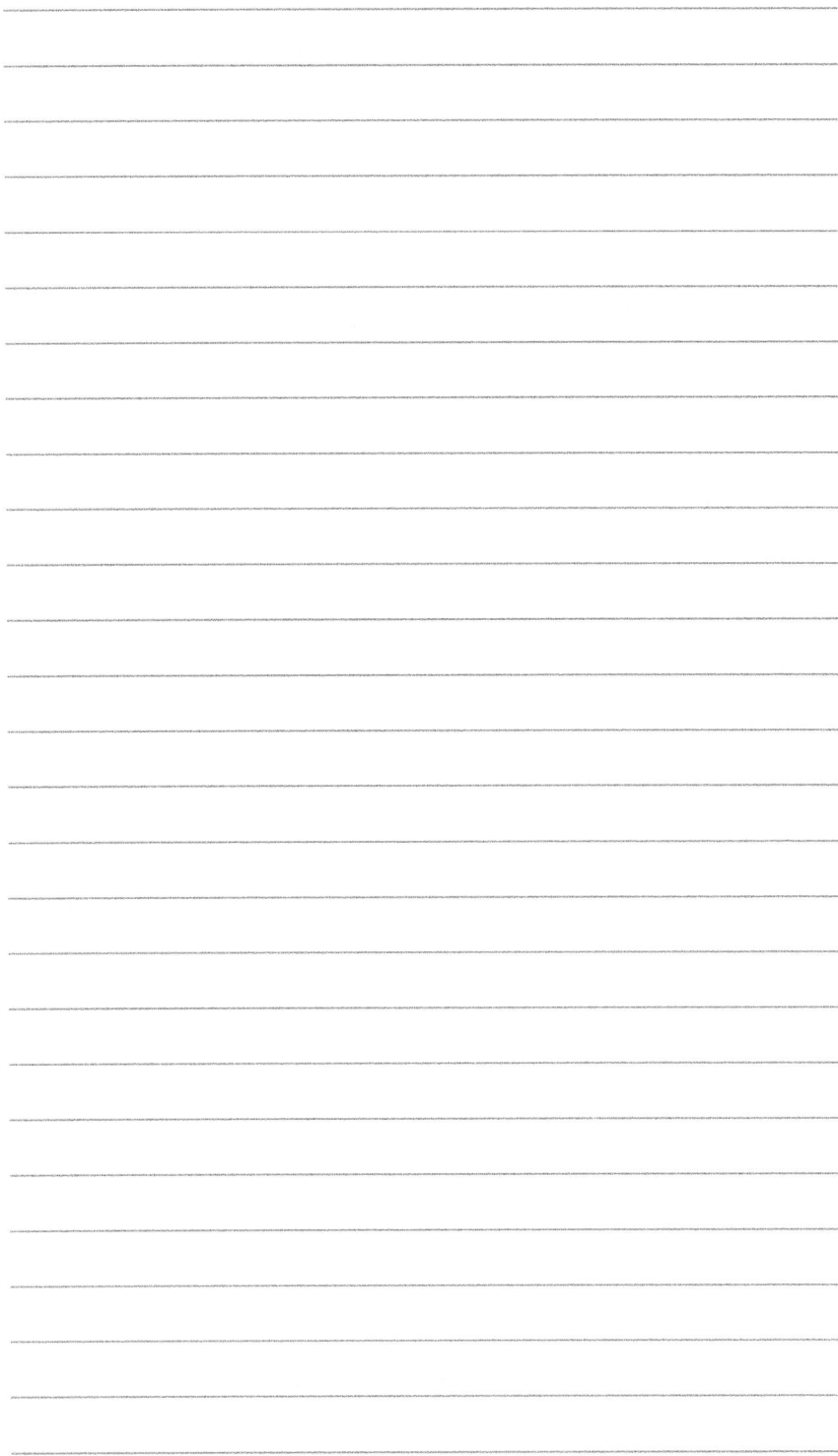

About the Author

Ace Doligosa was born on August 26th, 1992 in Manhattan, New York and lived in Edison, New Jersey until she was 18 years old. As the youngest of five siblings, she is the second to graduate college with a Bachelors in Communications at St. John's University. Since then, she has sustained strong relationships in media, entertainment, politics, technology, and entrepreneurialism.

Notable Executives, Producers, and Public Figures she has worked with are Susan Jin Davis, Sallie Schoneboom, Cubby Bryant, and Alex Ditrolio, many of whom work or worked at companies such as iHeartRadio, SiriusXM, Comcast NBCUniversal Inc. and CAA.

At an early age, Ace had thoughts of suicide and found that suicidal thoughts were not uncommon amongst her communities. Throughout her experiences, she found that she was not alone in her struggles. In 2017, TIME Magazine reported that public-health groups discovered that 36,000 millennials died due to "deaths of despair." As a minority millennial who overcame adversity from discrimination, public mental health negligence, immigration challenges, and financial obstacles, she now serves as an Artist, Mental Health Awareness Advocate, and Entrepreneur.

www.ingramcontent.com/pod-product-compliance
Lightning Source LLC
Chambersburg PA
CBHW070439100426
42812CB00031B/3339/J